THOMAS JOSHUA COOPER

THE RIM OF GLASGOW
"Hidden Views"
Part one of a two-part work

Ballagan Glen
Old Stirlingshire
Scotland, 1988

ART IN THE GARDEN

Edited and produced by

GRAEME MURRAY
EDINBURGH

FOR

GLASGOW GARDEN FESTIVAL 1988 LTD.

SPONSORED BY

THE ROYAL BANK OF SCOTLAND

Other sponsors involved in the visual arts programme are: Art in Partnership Scotland, Co-operative Wholesale Society Ltd., Forestry Commission, Calouste Gulbenkian Foundation, Henry Moore Foundation, Institüt für Auslandesbezeihunger, Kunsthaus, Nürnberg, Open Circle Scotland Ltd., Scottish Arts Council, Scottish Sculpture Trust, Sky Marble, University of Glasgow, & The Third Eye Centre.

ISBN 0948274 018

PRINTED IN THE NETHERLANDS BY LECTURIS B.V.
PHOTOGRAPHS BY DAVID HAZEL AND RICHARD LEAROYD
Other photographic credits: Guthrie Photography, Murdo McLeod, The South Bank Centre

FRONT COVER — Linda Taylor, "Unseen Current", 1988

ART IN THE GARDEN

INSTALLATIONS

GLASGOW GARDEN FESTIVAL

Glasgow
Garden Festival '88

GRAEME MURRAY
EDINBURGH
MXIIM

The Royal Bank of Scotland

PREFACE

Isabel Vasseur

SINCE Liverpool in 1984 and Stoke in 1986, the Visual Arts have played an important part in garden festivals. It has been the aim of the Glasgow Garden Festival to similarly bring an exciting collection of works by contemporary artists to integrate with the 100 acres of gardens and landscaping of the site. There is nothing new about artists' involvement in landscape and garden design, though it will be found that in the 20th century they have been somewhat banished from the public environment, populated as it is with Victorian statues reflecting the aspirations of another age. However, since 1945, with the revelation of the talents of Barbara Hepworth and Henry Moore, it was realised that there existed a new demand for three-dimensional work to be placed in parks and open spaces, and in 1948 the first "Open Air Exhibition of Sculpture" was organised by the London County Council. Since then sculptors have increasingly been invited to participate in the making of the environment to enhance and humanise urban sites, and to consider rural and parkland settings where the work has once again mediated and given scale to the built and natural world.

The Glasgow Garden Festival presents a wide range of opportunities which artists have seized with enthusiasm and imagination, overcoming, and in some cases, extending the original perception of their role in the Festival. In spite of the comparative lateness of their inclusion in the design concept of the site, they have succeeded in undertaking unexpected tasks such as architectural and landscape schemes which have necessitated collaboration with structural engineers, giving a new dimension to their work in an outdoor environment.

Many projects would not have been possible without the encouragement and assistance given by the senior design consultants of Gillespies and Partners, and structural engineers, TA Civils. I am indebted to them as well as to the Festival Company and the Scottish Development Agency for their support in a context which was focussed on many other aspects of the Festival and, therefore, needed a degree of trust and good faith. Thanks are also due to the site managers, Bovis Construction for their help in installing the works.

The Visual Arts Programme for the Festival has received very generous support from sponsors from both the public and private sector. This funding has enabled the artists to fully reflect the energy and optimism of the City of Glasgow and the ambitions and aspirations of its people. I am particularly grateful for the financial assistance received from the Scottish Arts Council, the Henry Moore Foundation and the Gulbenkian Foundation, the latter of which enabled collaborative schemes to be established between artists and architects. The Association of Business Sponsorship of the Arts has also substantially supported the commissioning programme with a major BSIS award in acknowledgement of sponsorship from Cummins Engines and the Clyde Port Authority, who are both first time sponsors of the arts.

Industry has been enormously helpful, especially with "in kind" donations, making available materials and skilled labour for projects, which by their very scale, would have been impossible to undertake in the artist's studio. The specific sponsors are mentioned against each of the works illustrated in the catalogue but it would perhaps be appropriate to particularly mention the shipbuilding skills and accommodation made available by British Shipbuilders Training Ltd under a Community Programme scheme where, with the help of British Steel, the four largest sculptures of the Festival were fabricated. In all, the wealth of traditional skills in Glasgow, the romance of shipbuilding and the history of the Clyde have inevitably affected the work of the artists. I would like to thank the many people involved in these industries for their tireless efforts to make these works possible.

Much expert advice has been needed for the fabrication of water-borne sculpture and we are grateful to Ian Winkle of the University of Glasgow Department of Naval Architecture for his help.

The process of selecting artists and their works at very short notice was assisted by the advice and help of the Scottish Sculpture Trust, the Scottish Sculpture Workshop, the Scottish Arts Council and in particular Robert Breen of Art in Partnership (Scotland). They generously gave their time and made possible a final list of artists which includes over 50 per cent Scottish participation. Thanks should also go to the Third Eye Centre who have been supportive throughout the project and who are presenting a programme of Performance Art to run during the five months of the Festival. The Collins Gallery, the Glasgow Print Studio, the Glasgow School of Art together with the Glasgow Galleries Committee have also been infinitely supportive of the Festival Arts programme.

With its long association with artist-in-residence schemes, the Forestry Commission must be thanked for providing financial assistance and materials for a programme of residencies which is being held on the site for the duration of the Festival.

We are enormously grateful to the Royal Bank of Scotland for making this excellent catalogue possible. The catalogue has been edited and produced by Graeme Murray and we would like to thank both him and Thomas Joshua Cooper, whose photographic essay is included, within the concept of the publication. The Sculpture Guide for the Glasgow Garden Festival has been produced and published by the Information Department of the National Galleries of Scotland and I am grateful to Timothy Clifford for providing this important resource which is available free to the Public. The contributions of Yves Abrioux, Dr Walter Grasskamp, Richard Cork and George Mulvagh are an immensely valuable element of the catalogue and they are to be thanked for providing, as they do, a critical and historical context to the objective of integrating contemporary art with a Garden Festival.

It is particularly exciting to have received the loan of the two Henry Moore sculptures from the Museum of Modern Art in Edinburgh and I would like to thank the Director, Richard Calvocoressi, for parting with these important works for five months. We are also very lucky to receive the last showing of the Gabrielle Keiller, Eduardo Paolozzi collection which, having been originally selected for a garden setting, finds an appropriate place within the Festival. Thanks should also go to the Fine Art Society for the generous loan of a cast of the Sir Alfred Gilbert "Eros".

The Visual Arts Co-ordinator's task would have been entirely impossible without the research and administrative assistance of the Visual Arts Assistant, Julie Radcliffe, who has carried out a massive programme under enormous pressure with singular energy and ability. I am also grateful to Annette Hardcastle for her collaboration on the scheme and to the Festival Events Department and its Director, Michael Dale, for patiently harbouring the Visual Arts in its midst. The often difficult and complicated task of installing the work was carried out by Graeme Gilmour, Neil Ross, George Potter, Neil Ferry, Cullum Sinclair, Stephen Beddoes, Andy Stewart, Adam Alexander and Ken Hunter and I would like to thank them for the many arduous hours they gave to the project.

I would finally like to offer my deep gratitude to all the artists participating in the Festival for their enthusiasm, imagination and enormous effort, making possible a significant visual arts presence in a situation which at times needed considerable patience. They have undoubtedly contributed to the success of the Festival and once again, as is the tradition of a garden festival, provided an opportunity for a far larger public to experience and enjoy the work of living artists than if their works were kept entirely in the reserve of museums and galleries. I would also like to include in my acknowledgement all the many artists who have submitted ideas for projects but for reasons of space and funding have not received a commission. I hope that new opportunities will have been created for them by this further demonstration that art works well in a public setting.

CONTENTS

THE RIM OF GLASGOW   Thomas Joshua Cooper   2
"Hidden views"

PREFACE   Isabel Vasseur   8

INTERVIEW WITH GEORGE MULVAGH   Richard Cork   10

FROM VERSAILLES TO LA VILLETTE: Yves Abrioux   17
notes towards a history of French gardens and
their ideology

INVASION FROM THE ARTIST'S STUDIO   Walter Grasskamp   20

THE INSTALLATIONS   23

MAURICE AGIS   HEW LORIMER
ARTISTS' FLAGS   MARTHA MACDONALD
KEVIN ATHERTON   TRACY MACKENNA
ROBERT BRUYNINCKX   DHRUVA MISTRY
JIM BUCKLEY   HENRY MOORE
SJOERD BUISMAN   PETER NOBLE
DANIEL BUREN   EDUARDO PAOLOZZI
MARC CHAIMOWICZ   MICHELANGELO
DOUG COCKER   PISTOLETTO
VAIRI CORR   WILLIAM PYE
RICHARD DEACON   RONALD RAE
IAN HAMILTON FINLAY   COLIN ROSE
KAREN FORBES   ARRAN ROSS
RAF FULCHER   MARIO ROSSI
  GEORGE CARTER   SOPHIE RYDER
SIR ALFRED GILBERT   BENNO SCHOTZ
ALISDAIR GOURLAY   LOUISE SCULLION
RICHARD GROOM   MICHAEL SNOWDEN
DAVID KEMP   LINDA TAYLOR
JAKE KEMPSALL   THEATRECRAFT
SHONA KINLOCH   WORKSHOPS
PATRICIA LEIGHTON   WILLIAM TURNBULL
JO LEWINGTON   GEORGE WYLLIE
ALF LOEHR

APPENDIX I   OTHER GARDENS   112

APPENDIX II   RAINBOW — A Proposal   114

APPENDIX III   Artists in Residence   115
                                Performance Artists

THE RIM OF GLASGOW   Thomas Joshua Cooper   117
"Hidden views"

WILLIAM PYE, "Balla Frois" (Wall of Water)

INTERVIEW WITH GEORGE MULVAGH

Richard Cork

RC: How did you get involved in the project?

GM: My practice was involved in the original feasibility study to enable a bid to be made to the Government for a Garden Festival in Glasgow. I believe there were about 50 entrants in the aftermath of the Liverpool Garden Festival. They were finally cut down to three and the Government, in its infinite wisdom, gave all three a prize. We tried for 1989, thinking that would give us a decent sort of time, but the Government decided we should have first prize and that it would be 1988. That announcement was made in October 1984.

RC: Does that mean the whole project has been rather a rush, so far as you are concerned?

GM: Oh yes. The timescale is desperately short compared with European Festivals. For example, planning started at Düsseldorf ten years before opening; Berlin had a twelve-year planning and construction period.

RC: Why do you need so much time, ideally?

GM: For two reasons. If you are trying to create a piece of parkland that is sufficiently mature to be a good visitor experience, as the Germans do, you need at least four or five years. There is also a fine balance to be reached between how much you spend in capital terms. One extreme is to buy very cheap material, as the Forestry Commission do, and stand back while it grows for you. The other extreme is to buy expensive materials for instant effect. We have tended to adopt this approach to offset the short timescale. If one had longer, one would probably do it differently.

The other point is this. Everything takes time to mature. With so many participants in the Festival, it takes time to negotiate designs and sponsorship. It takes time to get people warmed up, to allow people to fall out and be replaced.

There is not much time in a two-year cycle to make a mistake somewhere. Very little time to go back and alter anything if you don't get it right first time, or finding alternatives if you have set your heart on getting an artist to do specific work which then doesn't materialise. On the other hand, if one followed the German model, a lot of time could be wasted. They tend to spend a lot of energy arguing among themselves, and trying to re-invent the wheel. So there is probably a compromise period, maybe four or five years.

RC: What was your reaction to the site when you first went down to examine it?

GM: I suppose my reaction was twofold. On the site itself, plainly everything had to be created. The site had nothing on it at all apart from one or two buildings. It offered enormous scope from that point of view. You weren't constrained by a lot of existing features: you had to create them. But more important, we always saw the site as part of Glasgow. From all around you see out into the City. So the site is urban in its context. We have not tried to create something in an alien setting on the side of the river and the dockland where you wouldn't ordinarily get a piece of parkland. We tried to create a festive urban scene. So I thought initially: "There is a lot to do on the site, but the wealth of very interesting references round about will help develop the image of the site".

RC: It is instructive and interesting to compare the Glasgow venture with the two previous British Garden Festivals. At Liverpool, there was a very spectacular expanse of the Mersey which gave the whole event an air of immensity. And at

Panoramic view from the Finnieston Crane: Looking South East

Stoke, a vast amount of land beyond the centre was being reclaimed from the ravages of industrial misuse. Here it seems, something else again, lodged near the heart of a great city — striving to define a new role for itself.

GM: The Festival site offers some of the most dramatic views you find within Glasgow. The City does not have a hugely differentiating topography. It is built, as you probably know, as a grid iron plan on a series of drumlins. So you get a few silhouetted views, but generally speaking, the city is four storeys high with many church spires and towers. The view across the river to the Park area sky-line and the University, is particularly arresting.

RC: What do you do with a view like that — do you call attention to it, or create a prospect that will compete with it in some way?

GM: You draw your attention to it. The site has been laid out in such a way that the river runs parallel with the esplanade and this relationship has been left largely undisturbed. So a large number of people can look north and see the sun shining with this panorama in the background. There are one or two little jokey references to it within the site: elements that appear in the sky-line have been reproduced in caricature in the High Street area of the site.

RC: A mighty challenge is offered by the form of the Finnieston crane, of course. It's a hard act to follow really.

GM: That is why we have not touched it. In any case, we ran out of time to do anything, but that was the best solution of the lot.

RC: What was the first step in the creation of the parkland itself?

GM: Once we got through the initial feasibility phase, the first step was to completely revise the earlier masterplans and review the objectives of the Garden Festival. It

Looking South

Looking South West

was decided, after a great deal of discussion, that the whole event was really about having a fun day out for the family group. It was also very important that the project became a commercial success. We looked at other leisure parks worldwide, in the States, the Far East, Europe and various other places, to see what actually was their formula for success. We then produced a masterplan for the site, which used several of the basic guidelines from American theme parks.

Visitors arrive at a single entrance and they are then funnelled into the centre of the site — usually, though not always, through a commercial outlet of some sort. So there is a merchandising opportunity at the entrance. Once they have got to the central space, they can sample the festival in an organised way. Running in parallel with that, we decided to theme the Festival in terms of subjects that would be important and relevant to Glasgow. Important horticulturally as it is a Garden Festival after all, but particularly looking at its maritime influences or science and technology where Glasgow has been strong historically on fields where there are reasonable prospects in terms of industry and commerce.

After many suggestions, we settled on six themes: water and maritime, recreation and sport, health and well-being, plants and food, science and technology and land and scenery. We gave each of these titles to one of the theme sectors and together they make up the Festival experience.

RC: What does all this have to say about a vision of Glasgow in the future? I am very conscious that the Festival is happening at a time when Glasgow is struggling hard to regenerate itself.

GM: It was felt very strongly by all the people who promoted the festival that it had come along at exactly the right time for Glasgow. Three or four years earlier it would have been seen as a frivolous way of going about solving Glasgow's pretty dire problems. Since then the Burrell Collection, Scottish Ballet, environmental improvement and new development and investment have given this place a lot of confidence. Any later in fact, and we wouldn't have had a site to put the Festival on.

RC: You mean it would have been redeveloped?

GM: Yes. The site was planned for housing and the Festival Company has leased the site from the housing developers. So the event essentially is a temporary one. There has been no attempt here to create a permanent park, it is a Festival for five months.

Afterwards, it would all be taken away and the site developed for housing. Needless to say many people felt this was wrong, that so much effort should not go into something entirely temporary but others believed that time would change things and so it has. Now what will happen is that part of the site will be developed for housing and part of it will stay as a park. Part of the riverfront linked by the footbridge to the SECC, will stay as a permanent leisure area and part will become a business park in which much of the landscape will remain.

RC: Have there been many criticisms that this is not what Glasgow needs — that it is only a superficial showbiz exercise?

GM: No. I think most people grasped what it was about, although some still misunderstand the concept of the Garden Festival. I have come across very few people who view it as a waste of money or time. However, quite a number condemned the temporary nature of the event but I think they will now be pleased with the change that has been negotiated. Given a successful event, there may well be further revisions. Issues like this take time to resolve. Liverpool,

Looking East

GEORGE WYLLIE: "Straw Locomotive"

you might recall, was to be virtually cleared away and it is mostly still there four and half years later.

RC: Looking back at the Festival of Britain in 1951 which can be seen as the great forerunner of these recent ventures, it seems tragic that everything was swept away apart from the Royal Festival Hall.

GM: Yes, particularly in view of what was subsequently built on the site! That was a totally wasted opportunity. Glasgow has a tremendously strong tradition in Exhibition terms, so we would trace our links back further than 1951. We go back to the 1888 Jubilee Exhibition, which created Kelvingrove Art Gallery and Kelvin Park, and then the 1938 Empire Exhibition of which only one building remains in Bellahouston Park. That attracted over 13 million people and it was a huge success remembered by many people alive today.

So Glaswegians see the Festival in that historical context and believe it will be successful. They think that it is the right thing to do. They are also quite happy at the moment to have this sort of gloss on the City, having suffered for so many years the insults of being the worst at everything; the worst health record, worst housing, worst crime rate. But to be thought of as the best cultural city in 1990 gives one the belief that many such events could follow in sequence. Some people are now discussing what happens in 1992 and whether we can have the Olympics.

RC: You used the word "gloss" just then. Could it be seen to imply that the Festival is an event simply of the moment?

GM: Oh yes.

RC: Temporary, as you say, and of no lasting significance?

GM: I think it is perfectly possible to be both temporary and of lasting significance. It's main purpose is to bring visitors to Glasgow to show them the City and Scotland as a whole, in the hope that they reap benefits from that exposure. It is part of a huge piece of city and national advertising. A Flower Show like Chelsea for example, can be seen as a purely temporary event, but of lasting significance. I don't think it is essential that it has a permanent presence. If in the case of Garden Festivals, an effective piece of urban design or development can follow in its wake, so much the better. To a large extent this will now happen in Glasgow.

At the end of the day, we will reap a lot of benefits here. We already had a site which was going to be developed for housing, but in order to use the site for the Festival, several other sites were prepared, retrieved from a derelict state and put into use. Some of that work would never have been done — at least not in the foreseeable future — without the catalytic influence of the Festival. You can also look at the streets around the site and see stone cleaning, building repairs and environmental improvement, all carried out now because of the Festival.

RC: You are also restoring some rather intriguing old buildings on the site itself.

GM: Yes, we kept anything that it was possible to keep. There are three listed buildings on the site. The most important is the Four Winds pumping station which is Grade A.

RC: When was it designed?

GM: In 1894. It originally had a tall chimney stack. It was called the Four Winds because the tower was supposed to replicate the tower of the Four Winds in Athens. It's a very elegant building and we have carried out, what I would call, a stage one repair — new roof, wall repairs, new windows and a cleaned exterior. It is now ready to hand over to someone to re-use it after the Festival. And then there is the Rotunda. This is a Grade B listed building, one of a pair of pepper pot shaped buildings which sit on either side of the river connected by a tunnel. That again is a phase one repair and will be used as a restaurant during the

Festival. The third one is the Accumulator Tower in the south-west corner of the site. We had hoped to install a children's sound and light experience inside, but at the last minute we couldn't find a sponsor. However, it has been repaired and made wind and water tight. The pigeons have been chased out and barred for life. So again, this building is ready for some interesting and enterprising new use after the Festival.

RC: Above all though, there is a range of sculpture which punctuates the experience of walking round the area. How did you see sculpture fitting in here, what role does it play?

GM: Isabel and I talked about this a great length but I have to say that I don't actually think it is playing the role that it should play. It, by and large, consists of a series of imported works of art for which the best possible sites have been found. There are very few pieces here generated by the site or the event itself. You would have to start much further back in the design process to do that. I wish now I had the time over again and thought more about it earlier.

RC: Why was sculpture not considered to be an integral part of the project from the word go?

GM: The honest answer is that it wasn't thought to be important enough. Probably the link wasn't made between sculpture as an object and the artist as someone who could assist in the planning of the site. There are sculptors who could make a contribution to the overall design. They tried it in Berlin for example, where an artist was involved in the planning part of the site. I don't think the design team and myself realised how influential sculpture could be in the shaping of a masterplan. However, we do have a most interesting collection of works and for the most part, they add considerably to the visitors' experience.

RC: A good number have arisen from a sculptor's response to the site. For example, the Daniel Buren is very much the result of his visit to the area and his decision to capitalise on existing features he discovered there.

GM: We have a riverside site here with powerful forces of water rising and falling and equally powerful forces of wind. A few people have taken those elements and been inspired by the fact that it is a dockland site.

RC: That presumably is why Isabel thought of using the former crane plinth as the base for a larger sculpture and asked Richard Deacon to do something for it. The plinth does have a formidable presence in itself.

GM: I am hoping it will be sufficiently strong to overcome all the clutter. Ultimately, I believe it will be. You are quite right: it is an extremely powerful piece, with good strong proportions and very simply detailed.

Then there are sculptors who work with the natural elements of the landscape. We did invite Andy Goldsworthy here, but he declined. He felt the site was a moving target which he couldn't deal with. The constant change has been a very big trial both for artists and for all the designers here. The design has evolved as new pieces of work were introduced and it has been extremely difficult for some of the artists to visualise their work in such a changing setting. But maybe you could say that the site requires a particular kind of response from the artist, one which will accept the surroundings as if they were a townscape where buildings are taken down, new traffic routes put in, new signs put up, cafes opened then closed, a state of flux where their work might be. The Festival site is very much like that and far removed from a conventional sculpture park where the site can be guaranteed, the sculptor there knows nothing will intrude. At the Festival, unfortunately, we have never been able to create these conditions.

RC: I vividly remember going to the Liverpool Garden Festival, perhaps a couple of months before it opened, and being impressed by some of the sculpture already

Site Development, Autumn 1987

Looking North to the Campsies

on site. It looked very good in this unadorned setting before the site had been brought to its final stage. The sculptors had obviously done their best to marry their work to the landscape as it then existed. But afterwards, I went back when the Festival was in full swing and I was astonished and disconcerted to find how very different it was and how awkward some of these works now looked. I'll never forget finding the Stephen Cox carving, which had previously appeared very noble by a lakeside, and discovered to my alarm that a hamburger stall had been put up next to it. The relationship between the water and this carving which had once looked like a tree growing out of the ground, was disrupted by this gross intrusion — I couldn't understand how that had been allowed to happen. But I suppose it is one of the hazards of a Garden Festival where so many different activities are jostling for attention all the time.

GM: Yes, it's extremely busy and the real problem is that no single person has designed the site. We have perhaps 120 sponsors, each of whom has produced a design for a particular display area. We have done our best to remove the worst excesses: but it is really only now, at this late stage, that someone unused to reading plans could come along and assess the kind of context he or she could place a work of art in. I believe this presents a very great difficulty, especially for those artists who were introduced early on.

Of course, some pieces are so strong and so powerful that it does not matter what is being built round about. For example, there is a very strong piece at the Eastern Entrance by Bill Pye. It creates a focal point and provides a strong centre of gravity despite other features close by. Richard Deacon's piece, elevated on the top of the old crane base, and also I think George Wyllie's funnels, because they will move and clank and they are brightly coloured — attention will focus on those irrespective of their background. Maurice Agis's islands are simply so large that they will be the centre of attention. But the smaller pieces are more vulnerable. If garden festivals continue to depend heavily on private sponsors, with display space being designed by a wide range of people, this problem will persist. It may be overcome to some extent by having much larger sites, perhaps twice the size of the sites so far in this country. Then the conventional site — a large green place, or a very large piece of water where the environment is bound not to be changed or interrupted could be provided.

RC: I think the sculpture by Ian Hamilton Finlay seems to address itself to the whole notion of a garden and indeed a landscape, more than any other.

GM: Very much so — you're quite right to remind me of that. Finlay's was a very early proposal and it was inspired entirely by a countryside theme. It's called "A Country Lane with Stiles". Yes, that's got its roots right in the landscape. And it provides quite a private experience in the sense that you go through the lane with high foliage on either side. Very little intrudes above it. Sure, you see the crane sticking up, but I don't think that matters. It's a reference to the fact that his piece is really somewhere else after all — not in the countryside but in the town.

RC: In a sense, then, there is a high degree of landscape design in the Finlay piece.

GM: Oh yes, I think there's a huge scope for artists like Finlay and his associates. His garden at Stonypath is one of the best gardens I've seen anywhere. As a garden, not as a piece of outdoor sculpture. He believes very firmly in having close relationships between works of art, inscriptions, thoughts and landscape, and he has integrated it extraordinarily well. I respond very much to that, which is why I would have liked to have had one or two other artists like Richard Long and Andy Goldsworthy, because I think they are concerned with a more extensive view of the landscape rather than the concept of an object sitting in a landscape being viewed. The artist can actually change the landscape in some way, making a statement in the landscape, however temporary.

RC: So that from the visitor's point of view, rather than trying to find the sculpture, they actually discover themselves in the sculpture.

GM: Exactly, if there was a greater integration between the works of art and the landscape, I think a stronger relationship might develop between the sculpture and its observer.

RC: But you need a different kind of event for that, don't you? Something more clearly to do with art as a prime priority and less to do with the entertainment principle, which you described at the beginning as one of the overriding aims of the whole project.

GM: Well, it depends on whether you believe that art and entertainment have to be separated.

RC: I think the problem with the entertainment business is that, once those concerns enter in, they're very powerful. They tend to sweep sculpture to one side. People who think they know about entertainment have very fixed ideas and they are not normally to do with art.

GM: That is undoubtedly true, but the Glasgow event is not being run by Trust House Forte. It is being run by a Garden Festival Company which, despite the fact that it is promoting entertainment and fun day out and all the rest of it, is also promoting a whole host of other things such as landscape, horticulture, industry and design. Into that falls the whole art community, whether they are sculptors or landscape designers. Maybe in some instances no distinction should be drawn between these people. Indeed the Festival, I would suggest, provides an opportunity to do things that, in other contexts, may be difficult or impossible to achieve.

GM: It provides a chance to experiment. You can visit a sculpture park to see the conventional, the sculpture sitting in probably much better and happier relationship with landscape. But the Festival context offers a great number of opportunities for sculpture and other artists to be "temporary".

RC: One aspect of the sculpture in this Festival, I noticed, is objects which in some way question their own role. I'm thinking in particular of Marc Chaimowicz's furniture sculpture. Various works have rather a pleasing subversive element in them, making people ask themselves whether they are looking at art or something purely functional.

GM: That's quite true. I think people will actually use Chaimowicz's furniture. We've placed it in a very appropriate site where his "throne" piece sits on a rise, surveying the view of the city that I spoke about earlier. I can easily see people sitting in the chair surveying the Clyde and the prospect of Glasgow beyond.

RC: It's always gratifying to see an artist trying out something new rather than simply going through the motions of well-tried formulae.

GM: Chaimowicz came to the Festival through Isabel, as a reaction to a competition that we held for the design of street furniture. The Design Council ran the competition for us and they asked twenty designers to produce designs for a special suite of Festival furniture that might even be marketed afterwards. They all failed miserably, so we initiated round two of the competition and asked students at the Scottish Design Schools to enter. That was a lot better and we are making prototypes of each one. Frankly, it never occurred to us to approach the art community. So here was Isabel pointing out that "there was another group of people who could design furniture; they were not furniture designers or architects, they were perhaps sculptors and they could equally well have answered this problem". To me this was a revelation.

RC: The Patricia Leighton piece strikes me as a good example of a work that seems to be both rooted in the site and rising up out of it.

GM: Yes.

RC: I rather like that kind of integration, I must say.

GM: I do too, and I find the form strong as well as satisfying. It's extremely well related to the site. It's very organic and in a way the site is quite primaeval rather resembling a truncated cone. I like her work a lot, but I don't think she has worked in a context quite like this before.

RC: There is a great variety of sculpture here, ranging from the innovative to the traditional. You have classic bronzes by Henry Moore, one of which I notice is a cast of the figure he made specially for the Festival of Britain.

GM: I didn't know that, but it's a marvellous reference. We actually hoped to have had a contribution from Sir Hugh Casson who was of course in my position in the 1951 Festival. But it wasn't to be, unfortunately. Two references like that would have been very nice.

RC: Was it deliberate policy to have the whole gamut of contemporary sculpture here in one festival?

GM: Yes, I think so. Isabel is really the person who acquired the sculpture and aimed to have everything from very accessible student sculpture, that the average person could afford to buy, through to pieces by artists of international reputation.

RC: Does that create problems, in the sense that you are trying to impose some kind of overall unity on the project, and you're presented with this enormous stylistic range of sculpture? Does that make your task even harder?

GM: In some respects it does because we do have pieces here which were created for an entirely different setting. But the environment of the site varies so much that it's been possible to find, if not the ideal site, a unique site for each sculpture.

GM: They are to be seen, for the most part, at close quarters. We've been unable to arrange to have very long views: The Richard Deacon is one of the few exceptions because it sits up on a high pedestal at the edge of the water. So overall, I don't think there's actually been a design problem, providing it is accepted on that sort of level.

RC: Was the Jim Buckley Sculpture made especially for that site?

GM: Yes.

RC: Because it seems to me that he's taken his cue from the whole idea of a Clydeside setting, and the fact that great objects of machinery once inhabited that location.

GM: There are a number of artists who have taken reference from an historical study of the site. But looking at my own favourites, they tend to be more rooted in the subject of the Festival and the landscape rather than those which take their cue from industrial artefacts. It is of course a perfectly legitimate thing to do, but it's not quite at the core of the meaning rooted in the site itself. We have a handful of pieces that are like that and I think they are very successful.

RC: All this is happening at a time when the art emerging from Glasgow, especially by young practitioners, has attracted a great deal of attention. From that point of view, it's an appropriate moment to emphasise sculpture as much as possible in a Festival like this.

GM: I think so, and there's another event in 1990 coming up. We're currently trying to replan and redesign Glasgow Green, which is the city's oldest park. It should be possible to take some of the sculptural ideas which have not been seen in Glasgow before and find a permanent home for them there. At Glasgow Green, artists can participate in the redesigning of a venerable park, using some of the lessons that have been learnt at the Garden Festival.

RC: So you could see the present event as a seed bed for future developments.

GM: I would hope so. It requires someone to take up that idea and run with it. But we have a wonderful opportunity with 250 acres of parkland area.

The trees are all dying, the site will be completely denuded of foliage in the next 10 years. A new plan is required so what form of plan? What goes into the plan, do artists and outdoor sculpture have something to say about this? Here is an opportunity for something other than a conventional sculpture park.

RC: What would you say to those who would claim that parkland is quite beautiful enough in itself and has no need of art.

GM: In my view, that's the difference between an urban park and the countryside. In Scotland in particular, we have a lot of countryside that is untouched by anyone, the surface is barely scratched and you can't really improve on it. So the urban park provides an opportunity for man's hand on the landscape to be seen in a very accessible way. I think it's a major challenge of design. What is the 20th-century park all about, now that the reasons for the Victorian park have ceased to be? What sort of open recreational spaces should we have in our cities in northern Europe with its often inhospitable climate? The Parc de la Villette in Paris is beginning to show the way towards something new. Bernard Tschumi has designed something quite unique there and it is a lesson for the future.

GM: Some artists could play a very central role in this context. But they must be introduced to the subject at an early stage and they need to develop a working understanding of the vocabulary of architects, landscape architects and designers.

FROM VERSAILLES TO LA VILLETTE

Notes towards a history of French gardens and their ideology

Yves Abrioux

IF the great English landscape gardens of the 18th century drew much of their inspiration from major French painters, in the persons of Claude and Poussin, it is perhaps surprising to observe that painting has not played a major role in the history of French gardens. Once one has mentioned Monet's garden by the Seine at Giverny — so closely related to his painting, for which it provided numerous subjects (especially the famous water-lillies) — or an interesting but very much isolated example of a cubist garden, designed by Gabriel Guevrekian for a private residence in Hyères in 1926, nothing much springs to mind, apart from the specific and increasingly recognised role of Hubert Robert in the 18th century.

One may of course cast the net wider to take in contempory sculpture gardens, but to very little avail. The collection of statues by Maillol in the *Jardin des Tuilleries*, in front of the Louvre in Paris, is altogether too conservative an example of consensual cultural politics, side-stepping all the relevant historical questions by its obvious stylistic harmony: the mark of historical events has been eradicated from what was for centuries the centre of French power. Indeed, the French often seem incapable of gauging the historical texture of even the best surviving parks and gardens. A relevant example of this state of affairs is provided by the "sculpture park" (an English term barbarously translated into French) recently established in the *Domaine de Kerguehennec* in Britanny — a magnificent parkland setting two centuries old, aptly described to me (by a British observer, of course . . .) as "straight out of *Le Grand Meaulnes*". The arid modernism of the works exhibited there is for the most part out of place. Or else the forms and materials unfortunately evoke a spurious Celtic dimension. Aside from Jean-Pierre Raynaud and Ian Hamilton Finlay, practically none of the artists takes into account the rich texture of the setting. Nor does a militantly modernistic garden compare favourably. The *Fondation Maeght* at Saint-Paul-de-Vence, invaded by Miro's heavy post-surrealistic mythological fantasies, offers precious little satisfaction.

There are, of course, statues in traditional French gardens. In his guide to that most important of gardens à la française, his own domain at Versailles, Louis XIV is careful to lead the visitor round his prize commissions. However, the English were right to point out that the prime feature of the French style was its geometrical lay-out — what they stigmatised as the despotism of straight lines. Louis XIV's *Manière de Montrer les Jardins de Versailles* was intended as a series of instructions to subordinates whose task it was to show his guests round in his own absence. The various stopping places on the guided tour are carefully calculated to make everyone acutely aware of the massive presence of the royal palace. The visitor must forever have been casting a glance over his shoulder, to where the invisible despot might be watching.

The actual design of the garden at Versailles was entrusted to a gardener who as a young man had actually known Poussin. The son of one of the king's gardeners, André Le Nôtre lived next to the royal palace in Paris, and met the great painter on his one trip back from Rome in 1640, when he stayed in the Tuileries garden. However, Le Nôtre's main references were not to painting (it is not by chance that a recent monograph is included in a series on architects). Furthermore, the creation of a garden like Versailles was closely linked to contemporary technological advances, and to developments in geometry. Indeed, work on the Grand Canal involved experimentation with the latest surveying techniques.

Leaping forward more than three centuries, to the moment when the French state called for proposals concerning what is hoped to be a prototype for 21st-century urban parks, one finds a not dissimilar situation. Amongst French submissions for the *Parc de la Villette* in the north-east corner of Paris, one finds Michel Corajoud collaborating with the philosopher Michel Serres in a project based on contemporary scientific theories relating to the principle of disorder (in obvious philosophical opposition to the rational geometry of Le Nôtre). The landscape designer Bernard Lassus submitted a project for a Garden of the Planets, leaning heavily on the scientific imagination. The commission finally went to the architect Bernard Tschumi, who readily draws on the deconstructionist philosophy of Jacques Derrida. Derrida has himself been asked to look after part of the project, in conjunction with Peter Eisenmann.

One of the requirements stipulated in the *La Villette* commission was that it should be collaborative, so contemporary artists have been invited to participate. Daniel Buren worked alongside the French landscape gardener Alexandre Chemetoff on one of the few parts of the project completed to date, with Bernhard Leitner providing architectural and sound effects. This last detail is important. Chemetoff's bamboo garden occupies a section of the cinematic walkway (*promenade cinématique*), which is conceived as a montage of film sequences with accompanying soundtrack. Its "frames" do not invoke the traditional picture-frame, but belong to the contemporary art of the motion picture.

By the latter part of the 18th century, the French had of course felt the influence of the "Anglo-Chinese" passion for the picturesque. In the 1770s Louis XVI set about cutting down the century-old trees planted by his illustrious predecessor and replanting the garden at Versailles. The painter Hubert Robert was asked to record the event, and a few years later received a commission to revamp the *Bains d'Apollon* in the royal park. In the words of Count d'Angiviller, who was responsible for the king's building projects, Robert was expected to "give the *Bains d'Apollon* a more picturesque setting and appearance". A series of plans does indeed show Robert moving away from a rigid French geometrical pattern, towards winding picturesque paths in the English fashion.

One could not, however, expect anything of the deeper philosophical and ethical components of the picturesque in such a setting. There can be nothing, for example, of William Shenstone's *Semi-reducta Venus*, "encompassed round with shrubs" on his "ferme ornée", The Leasowes. In his self-imposed exile from the harsh life of the capital, Shenstone takes a sober line, denouncing in the inscription accompanying the Venus, both the gilded domain established by the French Sun King, and the alluring temptations of the east:

> And far be driven the sumptuous glare
> Of gold, from British groves;
> And far the meretricious air
> Of China's vain alcoves.

'Tis bashful beauty ever twines
  The most coercive chain;
'Tis she, that sov'reign rule declines,
  Who best deserves to reign.

It should not be forgotten that many of the great English gardens of the 18th century grew from a position of political opposition. In contrast, the numerous projects on which Hubert Robert worked around about Paris (and not, as was frequently the case in England, in far flung corners of the realm), were commissioned by the royal family and the high aristocracy, or else by financiers attached to the throne. Only the liberal-minded Marquis de Girardin, protector of Rousseau, seems to stand out a little from the set.

This doubtless explains why, for all their charm, Hubert Robert's surviving gardens do not have the same intensity as their English counterparts. The play on scale that is so decisive an aspect of, say, Henry Hoare's Stourhead, does not have as much impact. In the English gardens, scale is not merely physical, but also historical — the fruit of a complex sensibility mingling utopian and classical elements. The hollow in which Stourhead is situated is both self-contained and somehow boundless. The political sensibility of influential figures close to the throne of France could scarcely give rise to anything of that order. Could the meretricious frivolity that inspired Marie Antoinette's "ferme ornée" at the *Petit Trianon* at Versailles, a project in which Hubert Robert was also involved, be further from the English examples it aspired to imitate?

To arrive at a more satisfying notion of what the picturesque can provide in French terms, it is tempting to follow the example of two contemporary art historians. Yve-Alain Bois insists that painterly connotations are not so important to the picturesque as the extreme mobility it injects into the perception of forms in (or of) a landscape. The picturesque engenders an essential discontinuity, fracturing formal identity and providing shock effects such as are obtainable by montage. In other words, it quite literally implies a displacement of formal meaning, breaking with the dogmatism of French geometrical design.

Should such a suggestion not be pursued in historical, as much as phenomenological terms? It may seem curious that Yve-Alain Bois develops his theory of the picturesque in an essay on the American sculptor Richard Serra. Before finding a more permanent home elsewhere in Paris, a major piece of Serra's — *Clara-Clara* — was exhibited a few years ago at the far end of the Tuileries garden, where it opens out on to the *Place de la Concorde*, with the *Champs Elysées* and *Arc de Triomphe* beyond. Exhibited is of course the wrong word, for the effect of Serra's public sculptures is to modify our perception of their environment.

In the context of a discussion of the deeper implications of the picturesque, it is worth noting an observation made by Thierry de Duve, who has had the privilege of seeing Serra's work on both sides of the Atlantic. Referring to *Clara-Clara*, de Duve suggests that Serra's work is much more satisfactory in Europe than in America. The reason is that European cities impose certain bearings and imply specific directions, while American towns do not. One need only recall the work of Baron Haussmann in Paris to recognise the political and historical significance of this observation. The historical geometry of Paris' "triumphal way" was particularly relevant to the effect of *Clara-Clara* in the *Tuileries* (which should perhaps encourage us to confront the deconstructionist principles invoked by Bernard Tschumi with the philosophical dimension of the picturesque).

It is important to underline how relevant the precise siting of French gardens can be. Versailles was initially no more than a royal hunting lodge, but Louis XIV had good reasons for setting up court there on such a grand scale. By so doing, he succeeded in displacing the splendour of the sun in the geopolitical zenith, and in settling the traditionally fractious French nobles round a new focal point.

The garden at *La Villette* stems from a comparable ambition. Originally (as its name indicates) a little town on the outskirts of Paris, *La Villette*'s strategic position to the north-east of the capital made it an important centre for trade with Germany and the Low Countries. Architectural evidence of this remains, in the form of a rotunda built in the 18th century by the neoclassical architect Ledoux, to serve as a toll office. In the 19th century, Baron Haussmann was responsible for the geometrical lines of the canals which bound and cross the site of the new garden, laid out where the main Parisian slaughterhouses formerly stood.

In more recent times, the administrative and industrial pull of Paris has involved the lower reaches of the Seine to the west. The new garden is thus part of a long-term project to revitalise the east of the capital, which has suffered in comparison (new towns have been built in the Marne valley, and Europe's first Disneyland is to be sited in the area . . .). The three-tiered system according to which the park is laid out acknowledges its historical position. The gridwork of points at which follies are to be built takes into account the topography of the city, while the geometrical lines that are also part of the design have obvious links with French garden history, with tree-lined open spaces completing the complex formal plan.

The power-structure underlying the French garden tradition is thus very different from what was to be found in 18th-century Britain, where individuals used gardens to give themselves a place to stand in opposition to the dominant parties. This perhaps explains why the articulation between art and the environment in contemporary France is based more on the idea of the monument than on that of the garden as such.

The *Délégation aux Arts Plastiques*, a branch of the Ministry of Culture, has for some years been commissioning works of art for historical sites, as in the ill-fated project by Ian Hamilton Finlay and Alexandre Chemetoff for a garden celebrating the 1789 Declaration of the Rights of Man, at Versailles, on the very spot where these rights were proclaimed. Another site with which Finlay is involved includes a new urban motorway, an old-established tree-lined alley (evocatively named *l'Allée de la Reine*) and a municipal cemetery. The artist boldly uses this conjunction for a landscaping project with belvedere, on an 18th-century scale.

In north-eastern France, the administrative authority in *Champagne-Ardennes* has commissioned works to celebrate the four elements (earth, water, air, fire) at different sites in the region. However, so firmly established is the habit of multiple mediation, that this involves a commemoration of the philosopher Gaston Bachelard. A work by Bernard Pagès is already in place, and there are to be others, such as a project by Klaus Rinke celebrating water, which spans a canal.

It would be possible to list many similar projects. However, when a French sculptor shows more interest in confronting the specifically physical qualities of a site, important commissions are perhaps more likely to come from abroad, as in the major project Jean Clareboudt is currently carrying out with Robert Jacobsen in a disused gravel-pit in Denmark. Contemporary French culture does not generally perceive nature in such primeval terms, but rather sees the traces of human activity and history everywhere. Evidence of this cultural climate is provided by the attention aesthetic thought is beginning to give to a historian like Fernand Braudel, with his insistence on macro-historical structures interacting with geographical features.

The implications of such a situation are that the landscape of France as a whole comes to be perceived as a garden. In administrative terms, the landscape can indeed be classified as a "natural monument".

This has obvious consequences for the way the very structure of gardens is perceived. In an essay on Versailles, Thierry Mariage points out that French classical gardens are not self-sufficient entities. They transform the environment in which they are situated — a far cry from the enclosed paradise gardens of the Middle Ages, such as can still be seen at Villandry, near Tours, and also from the Italian gardens of the Renaissance, which had much more the appearance of a theatre set: they were to be seen from the entrance, with the main building centre-stage. With Le Nôtre, the palace or mansion becomes a launching-pad for the garden that is spread out below and extends its lines out into the countryside beyond. This is what makes it possible to suggest that there is, at bottom, no garden at all: just cleverly conceived transitional spaces leading (as at Versailles) to the forest in the distance.

The abstractness of such a conception can be discerned in contemporary terms, in the procedure followed by Daniel Buren. If Buren's work is "site specific", this is because he uses his standard striped interventions as a tool (outil) to act upon the environment, be this architectural or natural. Buren does not produce self-sufficient works with an autonomous semantic structure. As Jean-François Lyotard has pointed out, his installations must be read syntactically, and the visual, ideological or institutional repercussions on their surroundings followed through.

Bernard Lassus, who accepts that gardening and landscaping are impure arts, puts the matter into a different perspective. To find convincing models for the kind of mediation between a site and its environment that his point of view implied, Lassus left the beaten tracks of the official art-world and scoured the residential suburbs of major French cities in search of what he came to call les habitants-paysagistes. There he found a daring play on scale (and materials) not unsimilar to what the English had developed in the 18th century, albeit in an altogether different idiom. For the landscape designer the practical consequence was not only to enrich his formal vocabulary, but also to give his work a mythological scale. Lassus' designs, such as the justly famous project for the new town of l'Isle-d'Abeau (Le Jardin de l'Antérieur, 1975), meditate on history on a scale going back to the beginnings of life on earth, and effectively mediate between the values of art and nature.

Michel Serres has read similar structuralist fantasies into the work of Hubert Robert, while it is surely no exaggeration to suggest that the most striking and important of 18th-century French gardens is a fictional construct: Julie's secret Elysium in Rousseau's Nouvelle Héloïse, once again a philosophically transitional space.

The ideological potential of nature was revived in militant terms in the late sixties, when the radical support/surface group turned its back on galleries and museums, to exhibit (even in the most ephemeral fashion) in the countryside. Such a return to the basics of the visual arts doubtless suffered from the characteristic blindness of the avant-garde to the historical texture of its ambitions, and the dream of popular harmony quickly aborted. The fact of the matter is that the fête populaire, a politically potent mythical entity in France to this day, has a very specific history, going back to the Rousseauistic foundations of the French Revolution. However, it has taken a foreign artist, in the person of Ian Hamilton Finlay, to point this out in his Versailles project.

As 1989 approaches, bringing the bicentenary of the French Revolution and its cortège of emblematical liberty trees (arbres de liberté), will France see the emergence of a deepening understanding of the way history, institutions and ideology come together within the spaces we designate as gardens? Or, as the 21st century draws nearer, will la Villette fulfil the promise Derrida reads into the project, and allow a new determination of our relationship to otherness? The answers to such questions may well shape the next chapters of French garden history.

Coincidentally — or perhaps emblematically — this summer the grande halle at la Villette (whose survival owes much to the outcry that followed the destruction of les Halles in central Paris) will harbour Inventer 89, an exhibition of proposals for commemorating the bicentenary of the French Revolution. No state funds are to be provided for these projects, whose fate will depend on the availability of sponsorship. What will become of the landscape and garden proposals in the context of the "liberal" ideology of late capitalism in the 1980s? One awaits the outcome — on which the survival and indeed regeneration of a whole tradition in part depends — with a degree of trepidation.

SHORT BIBLIOGRAPHY

Yves-Alain BOIS, "Promenade pittoresque autour de Clara-Clara", in Richard Serra catalogue (Paris: Centre Georges Pompidou, 1983).

Jean de CAYEUX, Hubert Robert et les jardins, with a preface by Michel SERRES (Paris: Herscher, 1987).

Thierry de DUVE, "Au théâtre ce soir — drame en un acte et trois scènes", in L'époque, la mode, la morale, la passion exhibition catalogue (Paris: Centre Georges Pompidou, 1987), pp. 25–43.

Jacques DERRIDA, "Point de folie — maintenant l'architecture", in Psyché: inventions de l'autre (Paris: Galilée, 1987), pp. 477–493.

Bernard JEANNEL, Le Nôtre (Paris: Hazan, 1985).

Bernard LASSUS, The Landscape Approach of Bernard Lassus (London: Coracle Press, 1983).

LOUIS XIV, Manière de montrer les jardins de Versailles (Paris: Ed. de la Réunion des Musées Nationaux, 1982).

Jean-François LYOTARD, Le travail et l'écrit chez Daniel Buren, Cahiers du CRIC (Lyon: Nouveau Musée, 1982).

Louis MARIN, "L'Effet Sharawadgi ou le jardin de Julie", Traverses 5–6 (1976), pp. 114–131.

Monuments Historiques N° 143 (1986).

Parc-Ville Villette (Seyssel: Champ Vallon, 1987).

INVASION FROM THE ARTIST'S STUDIO

Why does modern public art come under attack?

Walter Grasskamp

"One can understand modern art
but not the modern world."
Werner Büttner

Science fiction

FOR years now, the Earth has been under the control of Extraterrestrials. Once their supremacy had been consolidated militarily and politically, they began to make their influence felt in the politico-cultural sphere. One element of their cultural programme involves erecting sculptures in the centres of large cities.

In Berlin's Mariannenplatz, they have erected a sculpture over forty metres in height and made of platinum. To the earthly observer it looks like an exploded colander that has been passed through a particle accelerator. Residents nearby claim that the monument emits perceptible rays which irritate the adults and keep the children awake at night. In the Cathedral Square in Münster, a thirty-metre-long iron plate has been installed which floats about twenty metres above the ground without touching it or being attached to any visible form of suspension. It is maintained in this floating position by means of a force unknown to disconcerted passers-by, and neither wind nor rain disturbs its equilibrium.

These and other places have been focal points for the protest against the Extraterrestrials' artistic red-cross parcels. In Münster a few inebriated physics students tried to disturb the plate's floating equilibrium during the night, but they only succeeded in jerking it some forty metres from the original site. The nearby post office was badly damaged during this attempt. They were caught up with and severely punished, but nonetheless achieved their objective, as their action galvanised a majority of the citizens of Münster to express their opposition to this ugly and incomprehensible construction in the form of a petition. The Westfalian State Museum was ordered to take the plate into its courtyard.

This was the Extraterrestrials' natural response to the failure of their politico-cultural endeavours — a failure they accepted with equanimity, especially as their political and military dominance remained unaffected by it. They even rejected a proposal from the Berlin Department of Culture which offered to create posts for art historians who, as so-called "Education Officers for Monuments and Sculptures", were to have shown outraged citizens the aesthetic value of Extraterrestrial art. What could have caused the Earthlings to react against this new kind of art in their public places, what is the reason for their unanimity? Resistance to the importation of Extraterrestrial art enables them to develop a feeling of being *Us-against-Them* which compensates them for the loss of their political autonomy. By refusing to put up with the art on top of the politics of the Extraterrestrials they make up for their continuing inferiority.

But if their resistance can be understood in symbolic terms, it is directed against works which are in themselves not symbols. As symbols they would have to be intelligible which, for the Earthlings, they are not; they would have to take a specialised course in the study of Extraterrestrial artistic traditions before they were able to classify these works correctly. In view of the expense involved, however, they ask themselves why these monuments are not simply erected where they can be understood without the benefit of additional study. Their efforts to understand fail not only in view of the possible meanings but of the style as well. Proposing to give the understanding an educational leg up in this respect completely misses the point that, besides the lack of explanation in the sculptures themselves, another much more important factor infuriates their opponents. It is an archaic reflection of the *territorial instinct* with which they defend themselves against the colonisation of their Lebensraum. The counterpart of this is the aesthetic requirement that, in erecting their monuments on Earth, even the mighty Extraterrestrials should at least respect local criteria of beauty.

Elitist scent marks

Now modern art is, according to all that we know, of thoroughly earthly origin. But don't the products of that art, scattered across façades, parks and squares of countless cities over the past sixty years or so, look as autocratic as the path marks of an invasion — not from outer space this time, but from artists' studios? Did it not spring directly from the pathos of modern art, to ignore the rights and requirements of passers-by and residents, or at best to fall short of their expectations? Didn't modern art's commitment to altering habitual modes of perception and exploiting preconceptions about what constitutes art give it *carte blanche* to do whatever it liked outdoors, as if the surrounding environment were nothing more than the soundbox of external sculpture?

Looking back on the still relatively short history of this invasion, even the most sympathetic observer must realise that modern art was not exactly predestined for display in public places. Its origin was against it, in the first place, coming as it did from a colourful, yet ultimately narrow and isolated milieu whose social profile owed less to élitist pretensions than to a mutual contempt for the bourgeoisie. Modern art, whose first breeding ground was in galleries, museums and private houses, *could not but* appear out of place in the public arena where the bourgeoisie — however vague their sociological contours, however unjust their defamation might be — are represented in far greater numbers than the supporters of modern art; they prefer a certain degree of exclusivity in any case. No matter how defamatory the definition of the bourgeoisie, however, it cannot escape the fact that an unerring instinct leads them to suspect modern sculptures of being monuments to the *cultural dominance of the educated classes*; and they do their utmost to resist these sculptural scent marks of an urbane élite. This resistance to the cultural colonisation of Lebensraum is the articulation of a territorial instinct which, over and above its archaic characteristics, is also the manifestation of a demand for cultural respect. Public sculpture, in other words, can also be understood as the *symbolic occupation of a place*, and the claim to sovereignty of this occupation is an extremely delicate matter given our democratic assumptions. Modern sculptures, encouraged not least by neighbouring architecture, also tend to assume proportions and contours which make them appear like monumental *gestures of intimidation* to the passer-by who reacts to them as his temperament dictates.

The mystery remains, however, that in the course of such debates and debacles, pretensions and contours are deprecated in monumental art which have been conceded with scarcely a murmur to postwar architecture and town planning — with far greater and much more disastrous consequences than art could ever bring about. In this one-sided concentration on modern art, one might see the setting up of a scapegoat to carry the can for all the barbarisms of modern life. Artists are made to shoulder the blame for this development since instead of compensating for the disfigurement of the modern townscape with intelligible, figurative sculptures that are pleasing to the eye, they make matters worse with monuments that are abstract, incomprehensible or brutalistic.

The silent march of modern art

But discussions about public monuments did not just begin with modern art. The 19th century, whose public sculptures are held up as shining examples by many critics of modern art, produced passionate debates concerning the erection of memorials and monuments. But these debates centred primarily on the local-historical or political significance attributed to the monument. When they did address the question of artistic quality, it was in the context of an unquestionably valid canon in which standards of representation and beauty applied which modern art dispensed with lock, stock and barrel.

Since the modern sculpture has taken the place of this monument without, like it, referring in clearly readable fashion to a collective, current body of meaning, it is treated as an illegitimate usurper and regarded as an insult. To get some idea of the provocation, imagine a demonstration involving large numbers of people marching in silence through the city centre without your being able to form the least conception of their objectives and motives, especially since the banners and placards they are carrying are completely blank. A silent march like that forms an appropriate analogy for the static presence of modern public sculpture which people drive past without being rewarded in the form of a decipherable statement for the attention these sculptures command. This, the symbolic barrenness of the autonomous sculpture, stands in sharp contrast to the strictly functional form of the environment. It neither conforms to this functional context, nor is it capable of visibly transcending it, as was the purpose of the religious or political-historical monument for centuries. At best, it is capable of disturbing it, and then it really does lay itself open to attacks in which the one-dimensionality of the townscape that is otherwise tolerated is confronted with aggression.

But the monument is not the only form of monumental sculpture in which modern public sculpture seems misguided. Its symbiotic relationship with architecture is even more problematic, having achieved a regrettable notoriety as art-in-architecture. 19th-century architecture still regarded it as perfectly natural to illustrate the function of a building in sculpture: lions in front of buildings used for political administration, the figure of Justice in front of the court building, statues of artists on academies of art and museums, half-naked stokers in front of the chamber of commerce and industry, half-naked Muses on the tympanum of the theatre and any number of classical quotations on institutions concerned with the preservation of tradition — all of these gave the public some idea of the buildings' function, just as caryatides, in the form of building labourers on the façades of town houses, indicated the source of the surplus wealth that made such magnificence possible. Today, while we may find the great variety of obsolete, innocuous symbols employed in 19th-century building sculpture amusing or touching, the fact is that this public sculpture constituted an intelligible and coherent concept of the town. Modern architecture has completely purged its products of this *descriptiveness*. Faced with many of the large — though not great — buildings in the modern city centre, we would be completely clueless but for the nameplates which tell us something about the function of the buildings. It is no longer possible to tell from their façades whether they are residential buildings, office blocks, student halls of residence, banks, university departments, hotels or court buildings. The intelligibility of the city centre is confined to the variety of inscriptions indicating their use for strictly segregated interests such as shopping, catering, entertainment, housing, services or administrative business. The intensive labelling of the city compensates *as text* for the lack of descriptiveness in façades and entrances, in the structure of the city as a whole. This non-descriptiveness, the result of an impoverished aesthetic, is probably irreversible in spite of all our post-modern illusions. On the contrary, it parallels a tendency in the development of modern industrial society which functions in an extremely non-descriptive way through a variety of media. This cannot be signified through any form of building sculpture other than, perhaps, the *logo*. Building sculpture has survived, however, in the form of art-in-architecture. But this, especially in its widespread abstract form, pushes the non-descriptiveness of metropolitan Lebensraum to intolerable limits. Since it cannot compensate for the non-descriptiveness or unattractiveness of the building it graces, it fails just as much as the autonomous sculpture that has taken the place of the monument. And since it is precisely this historical quality of descriptiveness in art which modern art rejects, it can neither structure nor transcend the townscape. It has ceded both of these functions, that of structuring to labelling, that of transcending the functional environment to advertising hoardings. Advertising spaces, as public altarpieces, graphically present the few universally valid forms of expression that make any pretence of transcending the context of traffic and trade. Without these functions, the monumentality of modern public scupture is seen as presumptuousness and it falls victim only too easily to the attention it attracts.

Locating

The very thing their critics interpret as failure can, of course, also be regarded as the strength of these sculptures, in individual cases, as an achievement consciously aimed at: the admission that they have no fixed cultural location.

It is precisely the *loss of descriptiveness* which constitutes the *symbolic content of modern art*, particularly in a public context. This, unexpectedly and paradoxically, means that autonomous and abstract art, if anything, would make sense to both supporters and critics of modern art, it would have a decipherable meaning derived not only from its own internal development but from its relationship to society as a whole. Its function, overlooked for so long, would be seen in its apprehending and demonstrating the universal tendency of industrial society towards non-descriptiveness, instead of giving it a more appealing and easily comprehensible façade as is the case with commercial and political advertising. We would not than have to ask ourselves any more why such works of art come under attack — the custom of punishing the messenger for the message he brings is older than modern art.

This sounds heroic and perhaps it is. Monumental public sculpture as an antidote to sense-stultifying advertising, as a disturbing element in the centres of consumerism and a spoke in the wheel of passing traffic — an argument along these lines carries such persuasive moral force that it can impart a veneer of legitimacy to even the most ill-conceived work of art-in-architecture. It was, in fact, brought to bear latterly in support of a work that is anything but ill-conceived, and more of a work *against* architecture than *in* it: Richard Serra's *Tilted Arc*. Benjamin Buchloh, Professor at State University in New York, argued this in favour of the retention of *Tilted Arc* in Federal Plaza, where residents had expressed their opposition to the sculpture. The conflict surrounding *Tilted Arc* is perhaps the most important and the most difficult test case in the dispute concerning public sculpture — and the role of the hero of modern art is tailor-made for Richard Serra. Heroic as this role may be, it is probably already history, too.

Abstract sculpture, which for decades gave rise to conflicts and campaigns in the letters columns of the press, predictable down to the smallest detail, this sculpture seems to have stood the test of time. If one analyses the signals from the relevant exhibitions of the past two years, above all the once again highly influential *Sculpture Projects Münster*, two new trends appear. The first, still few in terms of numbers but flourishing nonetheless, concentrates on *Service* — naïve, cunning or ambivalent. Scott Burton and Siah Armajani are the most prominent names in this area, an ice-cream parlour by Thomas Schütte at Dokumenta 8 takes it place with them, and in Münster's Cathedral Square, a complete bus shelter with portraits of Klaus Barbie and his defence counsel designed by Dennis Adams.

The other trend, widely represented, almost dominant, is the return of figurative or *narrative sculpture* which traces, illustrates or transforms elements of a *local iconography*. Jean-Christophe Ammann, Director of the Kunsthalle in Basel, and for years now an authoritative commentator on the problems connected with public art, sees a way out of the permanent crisis in both of these developments. What he has in mind is a kind of public sculpture that establishes itself below the threshold of perception. A classic example of this would be the arrangement of stone tables and stools erected by Scott Burton at a New York street corner. They have been arranged in such a way that their aesthetic significance reveals itself only gradually, perhaps never, to those who use them, even if they profit from their enthusiastic enjoyment of the work's artistic quality. That art, on the other hand, that is recognisable as such without wanting to be serviceable — painting and sculpture, in other words — that art is seen by Ammann in terms of a narrative charge to the townscape from which the clichés, symbols and monuments of an historical and local sense of identity have vanished.

Ammann's vision of a public art of poetic *conversation pieces* and fully conceptualised ambiences, Buchloh's defence of Richard Serra's *heavy metal* — these theoretical extremes of the current debate reflect the artistic extremes. But the problem will remain, regardless of which of these two tendencies prevails. The return to a figurative and localised public sculpture does not diminish resistance, in fact, in some places it actually increases it. In Berlin, for example, it wasn't the abstract works along the Sculpture-boulevard that caused the controversy — people seemed to have got used to them — it was Olaf Metzel's outstanding sculpture in the centre of West Berlin constructed from police barriers and shopping trolleys, and Wolf Vostell's car sculpture — two works, in other words, which are immediately comprehensible and relevant to a contemporary public. The conflict surrounding public art will continue, but maybe it is the job of this art to stimulate and define such conflict, so that a relatively harmless discussion can take place in relation to the symbol, of issues which, in reality, might well have remained unformulated.

Translated from the German by Michael Moohan.

THE INSTALLATIONS

25	MAURICE AGIS	70	HEW LORIMER
26	ARTISTS' FLAGS	72	MARTHA MACDONALD
28	KEVIN ATHERTON	74	TRACY MACKENNA
30	ROBERT BRUYNINCKX	76	DHRUVA MISTRY
32	JIM BUCKLEY	78	HENRY MOORE
34	SJOERD BUISMAN	80	PETER NOBLE
36	DANIEL BUREN	82	EDUARDO PAOLOZZI
38	MARC CHAIMOWICZ	84	MICHELANGELO
40	DOUG COCKER		PISTOLETTO
42	VAIRI CORR	86	WILLIAM PYE
44	RICHARD DEACON	88	RONALD RAE
46	IAN HAMILTON FINLAY	90	COLIN ROSE
48	KAREN FORBES	92	ARRAN ROSS
50	RAF FULCHER	94	MARIO ROSSI
	GEORGE CARTER	96	SOPHIE RYDER
52	SIR ALFRED GILBERT	98	BENNO SCHOTZ
54	ALISDAIR GOURLAY	100	LOUISE SCULLION
56	RICHARD GROOM	102	MICHAEL SNOWDEN
58	DAVID KEMP	104	LINDA TAYLOR
60	JAKE KEMPSALL	106	THEATRECRAFT
62	SHONA KINLOCH		WORKSHOPS
64	PATRICIA LEIGHTON	108	WILLIAM TURNBULL
66	JO LEWINGTON	110	GEORGE WYLLIE
68	ALF LOEHR		

MAURICE AGIS *b.1931*
Clause 29 1988
pvc & nylon 20 × 70 × 60m

ARTISTS' FLAGS *1987*

Flags by: Marinus Boezem,
Balthasar Burkhard, James Lee
Byars, Marc Camille Chaimowicz,
Luciano Fabro, Thomas
Kovachevich, Ingeborg Luscher,
Kunihiko Moriguchi, Meret
Oppenheim, Giulio Paolini, Leon
Schubiger, Niele Toroni
Musee d'Art et d'Histoire, Geneva

KEVIN ATHERTON *b.1950*
Swing 1988
mild steel, brass & enamel paint,
3 × 3.4 × 4.6m
Sponsored by Cummins Engine Co Ltd

ROBERT BRUYNINCKX
b.1946
Shelter 1988
galvanised steel & timber,
3 × 2.45 × 2.45m
Sponsored by the Ministry of the Flemish
Community, Brussels; Forwarding &
Handling Co, Antwerp; Sealand,
Rotterdam; Workshop for Plastic Arts,
Antwerp; Truyeus & Sons, Metal
Constructions, Antwerp

JIM BUCKLEY *b.1957*
Red Gates 1988
steel & paint, 8.3 × 7.5 × 2.2m
Sponsored by British Steel Corporation,
British Shipbuilders Training Ltd,
ESAB UK Ltd, Govan Shipbuilders,
International Paint plc, MSC & Murex

33

SJOERD BUISMAN *b.1948*
Phyllotaxis Scotland 1988
peat & steel 1.12 × 5.9m diameter

DANIEL BUREN *b.1938*
With George Potter, Graeme Gilmour,
Neil Ferry and Cullum Sinclair
Untitled: 170 Bollards 1988
painted, 0.59 × 0.09m [continuous
work throughout site]
*Sponsored by Delegation Culturelle
Française*

MARC CHAIMOWICZ *b.1947*
With Eric Coates, Ian Millar and
William Harvison
Philosopher's Set 1988
galvanised steel, wood & granite

DOUG COCKER *b.1945*
Sea Saddle 1988
galvanised steel 2.4 × 2.4 × 0.4m
Sponsored by Pillar Wedge Group/
Scottish Galvanisers

40

VAIRI CORR *b.1959*
The Golfer 1988, **The Swimmer** 1988, **Sunburnt Woman** 1988, **The Life Guard** 1988
papiermâché & chicken wire,
1.8 × 0.75 × 0.75m

RICHARD DEACON b.1949
**Nose to Nose, Beginning to
End** 1988
steel & paint 19.25 × 9.5 × 1m,
4 × 4.6 × 2.3m
Sponsored by British Steel Corporation,
British Shipbuilders Training Ltd,
ESAB UK Ltd, Govan Shipbuilders,
International Paint plc, MSC & Murex

IAN HAMILTON FINLAY
b.1925 With Keith Brookwell, Sue
Finlay, Annika Sandell, Thomas
Grieve and John R. Nash
A Country Lane with Stiles
1988

KAREN FORBES *b.1962*
Darwin's Spring 1988
fibreglass, patinated copper &
welded steel, 1.25 × 2 × 2.63m

RAF FULCHER *b.1948 &*
GEORGE CARTER *b.1948*
Folie de Grandeur 1988 nine
gateways and amphitheatre cover
decoration; wood & steel

SIR ALFRED GILBERT OM RA
1854-1934
Eros 1892, cast 1987
Aluminium, 1.9m
The Fine Art Society

ALISDAIR GOURLAY *b.1964*

Three Acrobats 1988
fibreglass, steel & paint,
1.8 × 1.2 × 0.3m
The Mushroom Men 1988
fibreglass, steel & paint,
2.7 × 1.2 × 0.3m

RICHARD GROOM *b.1962*
Floating Head 1988
cement on steel armature,
7.8 × 2.5 × 3.3m
Sponsored by BRC Co Ltd, British
Shipbuilders Training Ltd, ESAB UK Ltd,
Govan Shipbuilders, International Paint plc,
MSC & Murex

DAVID KEMP
The Ancient Forester 1987
oak, European larch & steel, 3.6m
Sponsored by The Forestry Commission

58

JAKE KEMPSALL *b.1940*
Flower Head II 1983
slate & stone, 1.68 × 1.63 × 1.42m
The Artist

Dark Flower 1988
slate & stone, 0.4 × 3.6m diameter
The Artist

Flower Piece III 1988
slate, stone & wood, 1.7 × 2.7 × 3.3m
The Artist

SHONA KINLOCH *b.1962*
Seven Glasgow Dogs 1988
cement fondue on steel armature,
1.2 × 0.75 × 0.5m
Sponsored by British Shipbuilders Training
Ltd, ESAB UK Ltd, Govan Shipbuilders, MSC & Murex

62

PATRICIA LEIGHTON *b.1950*
With Terry Jackson
Meall a'Chàirn 1988
(Mound of the Cairn)
site specific installation; stone filled
gabians, wood, turf & shrubs
ramp 4.5 × 11.5 × 2.8m,
seats 1.3 × 2.3 × 0.5m

JO LEWINGTON *b.1937*
Three Corbies 1987
cement on steel armature,
1 × 2.1 × 1m
Sponsored by Makro Self-Service
Wholesalers Ltd

ALF LOEHR *b.1957*

Recitation 1988
galvanised steel & aero engine parts,
8 × 0.4 × 0.4m
Sponsored by Rolls Royce plc &
Ciba-Geigy Plastics

Recitation 1988
copper & wood
Sponsored by Rolls Royce plc

HEW LORIMER b.1907
Ceres 1966
blaxter free stone, 1.8 × 0.6 × 0.4m
Sir William McEwan Younger
Installation sponsored by Scottish &
Newcastle Breweries plc

MARTHA MACDONALD
b.1962

The Pineapple Piece 1985
terracotta & enamels,
0.5 × 0.5 × 0.5m
The Artist

The Dress 1985
terracotta & enamels,
1.1 × 0.7 × 0.8m
The Artist

Victorian Standard 1985
terracotta & enamels,
1.4 × 0.7 × 0.7m
The Artist

TRACY MACKENNA *b.1963*
If Crocodiles Flew on
Wings . . .
steel, 2.7 × 2.1 × 1.5m
The Artist

DHRUVA MISTRY *b.1957*
Reclining Woman 1988
cement on steel armature,
2.3 × 2.2 × 3.9m
*Sponsored by British Shipbuilders Training
Ltd, ESAB UK Ltd, Govan Shipbuilders,
MSC & Murex*

HENRY MOORE OM RA *1898–*
1986
Reclining Figure 1951
bronze, 1.1 × 2.2 × 0.73m
Scottish National Gallery of Modern Art,
Edinburgh

Reclining Figure No. 2 1960
bronze, 1.2 × 2.6 × 1m
Scottish National Gallery of Modern Art,
Edinburgh

PETER NOBLE *b.1953*
Cover 1988
mixed media, 2.1 × 9.1 × 1.2m
Sponsored by Marbond Ltd

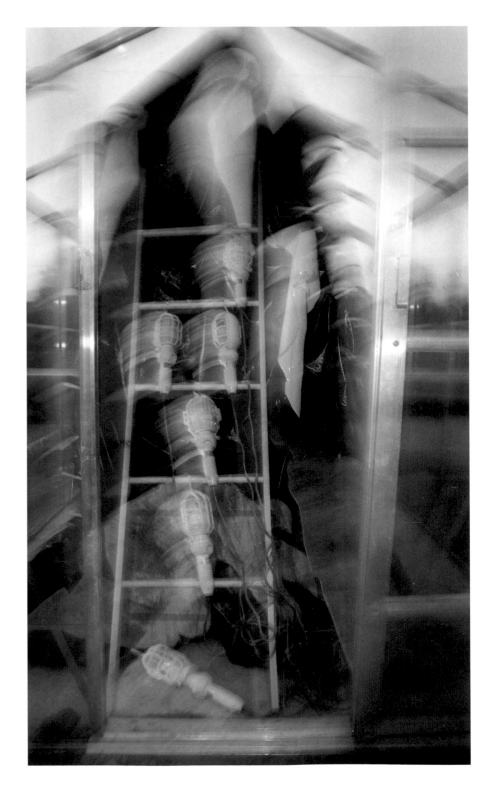

EDUARDO PAOLOZZI b.1924
Sculptures from a Garden
The South Bank Centre

Large Frog (New Version)
1958
bronze, 0.7 × 0.8 × 0.8m
Gabrielle Keiller

Tim's Boot 1971
bronze, 0.5 × 0.2 × 0.6m
Gabrielle Keiller

Rio 1964–5
bronze, six sections 2.4m
*Hunterian Art Gallery, University of
Glasgow*

MICHELANGELO
PISTOLETTO *b.1933*
Leoncini 1984
marble, 2.5 × 1 × 3m
The Artist
Sponsored by Fiat Auto UK Ltd &
Instituto Italiano di Cultura

WILLIAM PYE *b.1938*
Balla Frois (Wall of Water)
1988
stainless steel, 4.5 × 10.2 × 32m
Sponsored by Clyde Port Authority

RONALD RAE *b.1946*
The Shepherd 1987
stone, 1.5 × 1.4 × 1.3m
The Artist

Sheep 1987
stone, 0.9 × 1.5 × 1.2m
The Artist

COLIN ROSE b.1951
Rolling Moon 1988
stainless steel, 10 × 25m diameter
Sponsored by Association for Business
Sponsorship of the Arts, British Steel
Corporation (Tubes Division), Federation
Brewery, International Paint plc,
Moulem Northern, Metal Spinners
(Newcastle) Ltd, Northern Arts & Spartan
Redheigh Ltd

ARRAN ROSS *b.1965*
The Meeting Place 1986
wood, 4 × 3.7 × 3.7m
The Artist

MARIO ROSSI *b.1958*
Glasgow 1988
bronze, 1.2 × 1m diameter

SOPHIE RYDER *b.1963*
Fighting Stags
wire & paint, 0.9 × 0.9 × 3m

96

BENNO SCHOTZ
1891–1984
Moses–The Sculptor 1949
sandstone, 0.9 × 0.4 × 2.2m
The Trustees of Benno Schotz

LOUISE SCULLLION *b.1966*
Reconnaissance Bench 1988
steel & cotton, 1.2 × 1 × 2.1m

MICHAEL SNOWDEN
The Royal Bank of Scotland
Fountain
bronze, 7.1 × 3.3m diameter
The Royal Bank of Scotland

LINDA TAYLOR *b.1959*
Unseen Current 1988
copper, 1.5 × 0.25 × 16.5m

THEATRECRAFT
WORKSHOPS
Scarecrows
Fabricated by mentally handicapped
adults and people with physical
disabilities

WILLIAM TURNBULL *b.1922*
Totemic Figure 1957
bronze & stone, 1.54 × 0.43 × 0.35m
The Artist

Ripple 1966
stainless steel, approx 2.25m
The Artist

GEORGE WYLLIE *b.1921*
Arrivals and Sailings 1988
steel & rope
This sculpture was made possible by an
award under the Government's Business
Sponsorship Incentive Scheme,
administered by the Association for
Business Sponsorship of the Arts and made
in recognition of sponsorship by Clyde
Port Authority and Cummins Engine Co
Ltd

APPENDIX I

THE ITALIAN GARDEN
Franco Zagari
◄ Silvia Falconi
Fabio di Carlo
▼

THE IRISH GARDEN
Costin's Grass Garden
Tree Spirit, elm — Dick Joynt   ►

113

SOUTH.

SUNS RAYS

SEARCHLIGHT RAYS

MIST

MIST

42°

OFF

ON

UP ON DECK, DOWN THE HOLD, ROUND THROUGH THE WHEELHOUSE & OFF THE OTHER SIDE.

RAINBOW — A PROPOSAL

Ron Haselden

RON HASELDEN worked with DAVID PANTON and Dr KEN SMITH of the Physics Department of Glasgow University.

The idea for this project was stimulated by a boat trip on the Clyde. The weather conditions were dramatic with strong sunlight, rain and cloud. Near Greenock a large rainbow formed out of misty cloud and reached out across the river. It was this sight that prompted my idea for the Garden Festival.

A cargo ship is moored in the Canting Basin Dock on the festival site. The hold will be filled with billowing clouds of misty spray with fine droplets of water refracting the sunlight or the light from a searchlight and forming a large rainbow inside. The public will have access to this, where it will be seen in an environment that is normally the reserve of seamen. Each individual will see their own rainbow as it forms in relationship to their position with the light source.

Experiments in the Physics Department at Glasgow University have revealed very beautiful and subtle effects with the rainbow suspended in clouds of fine water droplets.

Two ships, which traded locally to the Western Isles, were found, but financial resources were not enough to cover the work and so it remains as a script. Fortunately there is much interest in the project and it could be eventually realised elsewhere.

APPENDIX III

ARTISTS IN RESIDENCE:
Mary Bourne
Sybille von Halem
Alex Hartley
David Howie
John Hunter
Rosie Leventon
Valerie Pragnell
David McMillan
Alan Watson

PERFORMANCE ARTISTS:
Bow Gamelon Ensemble
Centre Ocean Stream
Forkbeard Fantasy
Alastair Snow
Stephen Taylor Woodrow
Sylvia Ziranek

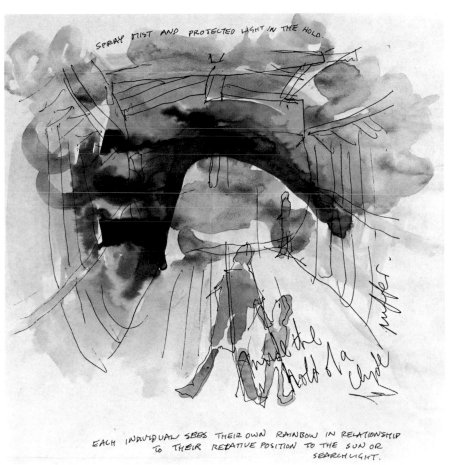

EACH INDIVIDUAL SEES THEIR OWN RAINBOW IN RELATIONSHIP TO THEIR RELATIVE POSITION TO THE SUN OR SEARCHLIGHT.

THOMAS JOSHUA COOPER

THE RIM OF GLASGOW   Dumgoyne
  "Hidden Views"   Old Stirlingshire
Part two   Scotland, 1988

117